D1710790

Nomi & Brave

Travel The Universe

WRITTEN BY

Sara Rodewald & Emily Rodewald

Saraisms Press

This Book Belongs to:

ELIZA

Auntie Cyndee
&
Uncle Lumli

I'm Nomi! And this is my
stuffed bunny and best friend, Brave.

Brave and I are taking our rocketship
through space and exploring
ALL the planets in our solar system.

Do you want to come with us?!

Let's GO!

Rocket stop!

It's getting **HOT**!

That star so bright

Gives us light.

Must be the SUN

Moving and grooving,
this planet is **FAST**!
Glad it is first
And not the last.

Must be MERCURY

Wow, what a sight!

So beautiful & **BRIGHT**.

You can see her warm glow.

Look out your window!

2

Must be Venus.

I know this one!
This is my HOME.
Filled with Mommies & Daddies
And a bed of my own.

Must be Earth.

3

A RED planet next door!
The one we'll explore.
I hope some day,
We come over and play.

Must be Mars

Fly through the asteroids!
We'll zag and we'll zig.
To get to the planet
That's ever so **BIG**

Must be Jupiter

5

Well here's something new!

I just want to sing.

Brave, do you see?

This planet has RINGS!

Must be Saturn.

6

Shhh...Rocking **GENTLY**
with a soft warm glow
This planet is sleeping.
We should go.

Must be Uranus.

This one's peculiar
And not very familiar.
Quick, grab your mask.
This planet has **GAS**!

Must be Neptune

Oh how cute!

Such a **LITTLE** guy.

Brave, look!

He's just like you and I.

Must be Pluto

Good Night, my friend.
I hope you had fun!
When you dream tonight,
Dream of the Sun.

CPSIA information can be obtained
at www.ICGtesting.com
Printed in the USA
LVHW071028030821
694405LV00002B/13